Try this!

- Glue small colored rocks onto the stained glass windows.
- Trace the bushes onto green felt. Cut out and glue on.
- Use glitter paint in a bottle or tube to make bell clappers shine.

Rejoice
in the Lord.
Psalm 97:12, ICB

Try this!

- Glue on real watermelon seeds (while enjoying a watermelon snack).
- Sponge paint red fruit and color the rind with bright markers.
- Add a small pom-pom nose to each watermelon slice.

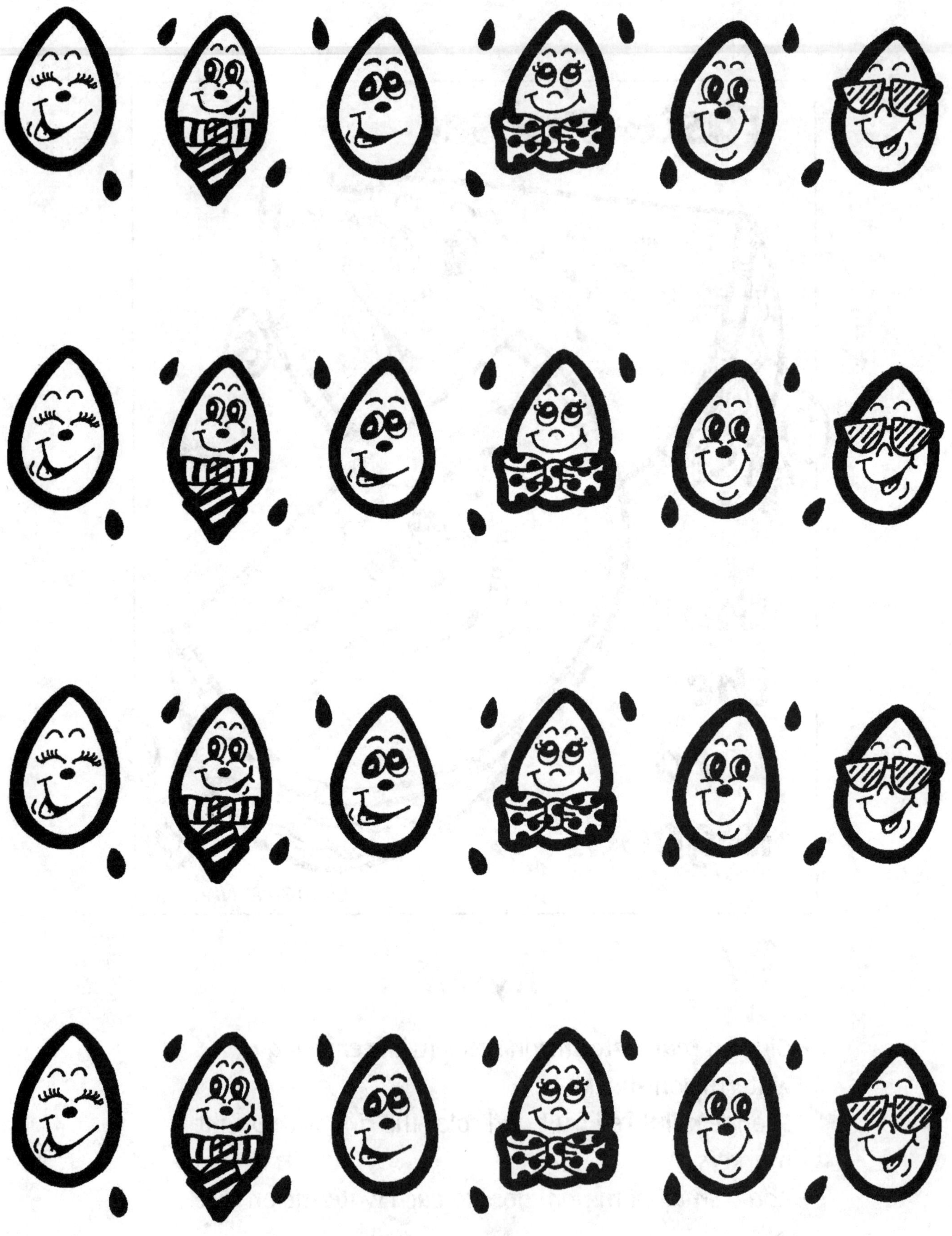

Taste and see

that
the
Lord
is good.

Psalm 34:8, NIV

Try this!

- Add fine sand to light brown tempera paint and brush onto the beach.
- Trace the palm branches onto green felt. Cut out and glue onto the chart.
- Use an ink pad to place a fingerprint on each heel. Observe the uniqueness of each person's print.

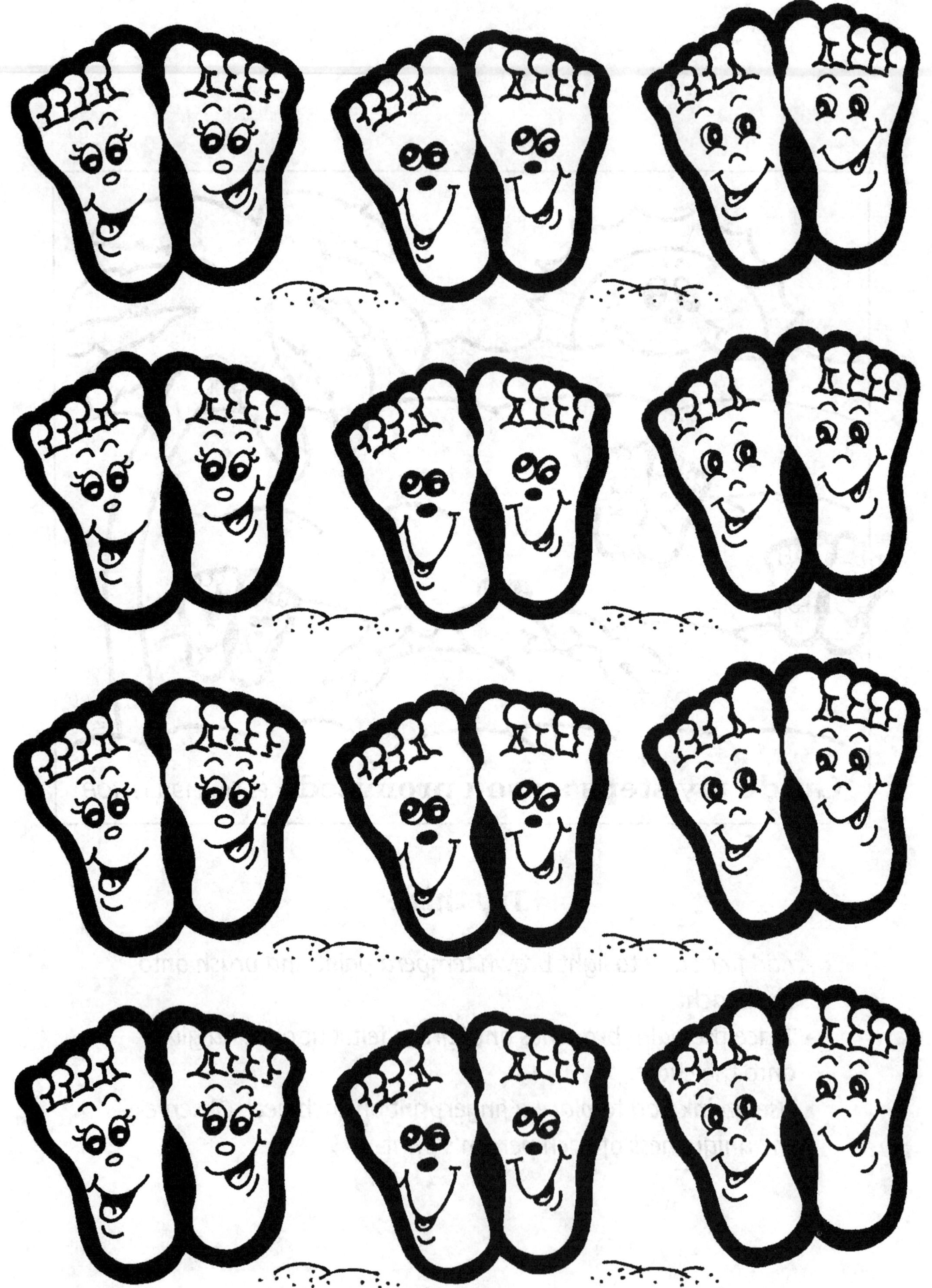

Guide my steps as you promised. Psalm 119:133, ICB

Try this!

- Glue rickrack onto the angel's robe cuff and hem.
- Add cotton batting to the clouds.
- Sprinkle glitter on wings and halo.

Make a joyful noise

unto the Lord.

Psalm 100:1

The harvest is plentiful.

Try this!

- Dissolve three parts dry grape gelatin in one part hot water. Use as paint to color and scent grapes.
- Glue wiggle eyes onto leaves.
- Trace leaf veins with white glue. Sprinkle with green sand.

The harvest is plentiful.

Luke 10:2, NIV

Try this!

- Fill in notes with decorative colored glue or add powdered tempera paint to white glue.
- Cover the tree branch with small wads of brown tissue paper.
- Trace leaves onto green tissue paper. Cut out and attach with glue.

Sing for Joy to the Lord.
Psalm 95:1, NIV

Try this!

- Attach wiggle eyes to the piggy bank.
- Glue on a curly tail made from a chenille wire.
- Before cutting out coin stickers, brush a coat of diluted white glue across the coins. Apply a sheet of yellow cellophane. Cut out stickers.

God loves the person who gives happily.

Try this!

- Photocopy bees onto yellow neon paper or color with neon markers.
- Twist four-inch chenille wires into springs. Attach one end of each wire to the chart and attach bees to the other ends to make the bees fly.
- Add fine brown sand to light yellow tempera paint. Brush onto the beehive.

Be kind and loving to each other.

Try this!

- Trace clouds onto white felt. Cut out and glue felt to the chart.
- Color with chalk and spray with aerosol hair spray to set the color.
- After the chart is complete, add clear glitter to the stars.

The
heavens
declare the
glory
of God.
Psalm 19:1

Try this!

- Place white glue drops onto tears and let dry.
- Sponge paint the bear.
- Put pads of pink felt on feet, paws, and ears.

Love
bears
all
things.

1 Corinthians 13:7

Try this!

- Decorate the Bible cover like one you'd like to have.
- Give the bookworms chenille wire antennas.
- Glue round pink circles cut from cellophane or construction paper onto the Bible's cheeks.

Lord, teach me
what you want me to do.

Psalm 86:11, *ICB*

God has made everything beautiful in its time.

Ecclesiastes 3:11, *NIV*

Try this!

- Snip lines between each flower petal to the center circle. Fold petals forward for 3-D flowers. Attach only the back of the flower center to the chart.
- Color leaves with colored pencils. Outline leaves and trace veins with decorative green glue or green powdered tempera paint added to white glue.

God has made everything beautiful in its time.
Ecclesiastes 3:11, NIV